Sudden Eden

Verandah Porche

*For Heide
with long delight!*

Verandah Porche

Verdant Books
Rutland, Vermont and San Francisco

Copyright © 2012 by Verandah Porche
All rights reserved
First printing

Designer: Debbi Wraga/Pamela Seymour Smith Sharp
Editor: Yvonne Daley
Printed in the United States of America by Northshire Bookstore
Cover photos, 1978, 2012 by Richard Coutant

Library of Congress Cataloging-in-Publication Data
Porche, Verandah (1945-)
Sudden Eden/Verandah Porche
ISBN # ISBN978-1-60571-168-3

Previous publications:
Poetry:
The Body's Symmetry (Harper and Row) 1974
Glancing off (See Through Books) 1986
Welcome to Total Loss Farm (Longhouse) 2006

Songs (with Patty Carpenter)
Come Over performed by The Dysfunctional Family Jazz Band

Play:
Broad Brook Anthology

Community Residencies:
Listening Out Loud
They Know the Promise
Self Portraits in Newport

YOU KNOW

WHO

YOU ARE

CONTENTS

1.

HE FELL TO HER KNEES

CLAIRE DE LUNE: 1945

Change pools on his nightstand. Sleep
eases down like a zipper, the "sliding-
pull-tab fastener" he finally patented.

Her dishes tilt dry. She plays Debussy,
pianissimo. Keys straight as teeth. Already
their daughter, balanced on a phone book,
can pick out *Happy Birthday*. "Little mother,"
she spoon-feeds the baby, frisky imp,
who grabs her hair and twists it, crowing...

The firstborn aims his telescope
and multiplies the leaves by galaxies.
A star pulls loose and lands on
his pajama shirt. The War.
She must reassure him.

Her husband saves his breath and spends
himself. She chooses fresh-frozen food,
the broadloom, their bedroom set inlaid
with walnut diamonds.

Tonight she slips beside his mind.
Ball bearings streamline the flow
of garments toward the loading dock.
In the pause of goods, he turns
to smooth her blueprint.

They manufacture me.

HE FELL TO HER KNEES

Copper like the teakettle
she hid in Minsk my mother's
mother's immigrant hair
fell to her knees.

She never invited her
daughter with the lean
obedient braid to touch
its river-fire.

My grandmother twisted and
pinned her pompadour as
corseted she bent to
the Thursday scrub

blacked the hearth
dissected the butcher
singed pinfeathers
for *Shabbas*.

She never wore a wig
when wed. No need
to be modest
for Grandpa

the tender socialist
whose revolution unfurled
his hands in her
feral hair.

SHE WALKED AWAY

Crone in an overcoat, she
hobbled by her double-
breasted sons.

My father's father knew her,
his prize producer: a baker's dozen;
bun in the oven, always.

She was the one
who "broke down." Let go
of our father.

Left him, a foundling
on Blackwell Island, to dodge
death, shielding

little Leo
(for Trotsky), his brother,
who did not.

"Dickensian," the script
in Yiddish
silence.

*

"Tell me, what your mother was like?"

My aunt emails from Florida...

> *Poison takes it out of me. When chemo is over*
> *I will give you tidbits of our history.*
> *Please keep a file as I have no printer.*

Months elapse.

> *Hello. My mother was a beautiful young woman,*
> *90 lbs. Had a wasp-waist when she married.*
> *(I never did) Anything she planted lived.*
> *The best operator my father had was my mother,*
> *called "Steam," because of her speed.*
>
> *I remember her hair, always pulled back,*
> *and her beautiful skin; her secret that never*
> *worked for me, to scrub until it squeaked...*
>
> *She rarely spoke of Russia where her mother died.*
> *...A pogrom or something...happened in her girlhood*
> *and she walked away.*

*

Maybe this: August 1880

Root vegetables for soup
jostle in her skirt. Daylight:
half-hour to the stepmother's hearth.

Nine peasants, red-tongued as dogs,
form a ring. *Hiss. Kiss.* Could be dancing.
Each with a stone.

She thinks nothing
of the weight her skirt holds.
Can't kill with a turnip.

They step close.
Tortoise-shell pins drop
from her unroped braids…

The skirt dries on a shrub.
Generations blanch
to mention this.

HEAVEN UNFASTENED

Two dotted U's
under a raw silk kimono—

mama's never-nursed-me
breasts rose, rose on pink

First, birth...
whiff, doze through labor, splay.

I blurted out, she woke sore:
voila, another daughter!

How did they
dry her?

Bottles and nipples bubbled
in the boiler.

Shirt shut,
she cooed on the sofa.

Her tilted words I sucked...
Hush, shush.

She fed
the formula.

KITCHEN SCRIPT:
SUNDAY, BROWNSVILLE, 1950

Cumulus in a house-dress,
our mother's mother hovers

over borscht and white fish,
the heavy relatives,

their Yiddish spit as, lovingly,
they chew our names.

The trombone man in the alley
with his weepy horn,
one never meant to play alone...

The pennies our grandfather
tosses down in a hankie
for mercy.

His walnut-cracking hands
hold out the crumpled meat,
and figs, copper, silver coins.

I study only store-bought
button candy dots: sweet, tart

Braille on paper strips.

Pastel yards of sugar code:
I mouth my Sunday script.

DEAR READER

Dad mows Saturday
after the factory and a trim.
I dance through the maze
the blades toss, X, L, Z,
and little letters in the grass.

Mom sews slipcovers.
The Singer hums.
Her knee presses the control,
a black steel
question mark.

When gravity gets to Dad,
we sink in, flank him
on the sofa she has gowned
in striped green velveteen.

He spreads the comic strips
and speaks at leisure. Index finger,
broken once and never set,
draws us through the painted boxes,
inky stories.

Our trance: with Dad, in daylight,
mimicking a gossip, a possum,
a thug or a prince.

FILLING IN DADDY

1.

Some kids were taught to keep still and chew
while we slouched over hamburger "campfire stew."
Sometimes *The Times* smeared ink on the kitchen table.
Instead of eating we'd think.
I leaned on your shirt sleeve and learned all the words
nobody needs to know. So today the peas never stay
on my fork the soup always sprays when I blow.

You'd say, "Tell me the name for a Philippine coin.
That's 22 across, the initials of Lincoln's Vice President,
an African weapon you toss. The Latin for 'I love you'
and the Spanish for 'divorce'."

Daddy. your gold mechanical pencil filled in every square
when the words never failed to fall into place
and my place was beside your chair.

2.

Later your hands shook. Letters jittered out of their boxes
and your own fatherly form shrank until it fit the final box
and disappeared across and down the past.

Most Sundays I still sit with *The Times* puzzle on my lap
and stumped I like to think you send back what
we've never seen: rivers in Romania Saturn's moons
and silent comedies: words you wove in me
that only show in late light like the pattern
of the shirts you wore: white on white.

HIS SATIN FINISH

Sparks
lit
our cellar:

wheel
gnashed
stone.

Alabaster
turned to
bone.

Dad
under granite
gravel sand

what friction
chafes
your hand?

MY MOTHER'S FALL

"Birds don't have to clean— the wind will do it for them"
Hilda Jacobs

How lovely that the birds don't have to
work so hard.
Wind rakes the trees till they look like rakes.
Leaves flap away. You

work so hard.
Just watch the evening steep like tea.
Leaves flap away. You
sit beside me on the sofa now that you're old enough to.

Just watch the evening steep like tea.
The stars are sugar which you don't approve of.
Sit beside me on the sofa now that you're old enough to
see they don't dissolve.

The stars are sugar which you don't approve of.
I'm rummaging around for memories.
See they don't dissolve.
With such a racket no one sleeps.

I'm rummaging around for memories.
Wind rakes the trees till they look like rakes.
With such a racket no one sleeps:
How lovely that the birds don't have to.

WITH MOM AT SEA

Arpeggios as surf: my mother's
   Beaked hands pick back toward Chopin.
      White keys froth against ebony pebbles.
   Her baby grand's the shape of a rock
You don't often see. A glacier sheers off

A massive slab. Salt cuts it down to size.
   My mother has a small bleed. One night
      She freezes, thaws and nobody knows what
   Synapses no longer fire. Once the water's
Frilled lace at Rockaway skirted her ankles

Like Mozart. At 10 she could fill her hands
   With sound. Be private even when the shore
      Teemed with good daughters like her
   On trolley holidays. My mother practiced
Passages on sand. Her fingers made do

With a cardboard key chart on the kitchen
   Table before they purchased week by week
      A piano. Eighty summers from that sea
   She leaves the brick home rarely willingly.
The glare hurts her laser-ed cataracts.

Let Venetian blinds divide the light in staves.
   Baubles on the chandelier fill space with
      Half and whole notes scored across the walls.
   She asks: *When did your friend come to*
Tune my piano? Were we over at Foodtown?

He did a lovely job. When I play now listen.
   My mother sets the beige receiver sideways
      On the table's plastic lace. I listen to the ghost
   Twangs of unvoiced strings. Chopin tosses
The piano overboard. My mother floats away

On its polished lid. Five states from her capsized
   Living room I catch my breath and dive. How far
      She swims my coaxing arms can't fathom.
   We play along shirring the foam. Only the chaos
My mother's joy provokes comes home.

SLEEP SPELL

for my mother in "the home"

August: money eludes us.
Leaf lettuce frills like this
chartreuse dress spirited back
from my mother's cache:
torn satin cut on the bias
too frayed to patch
too fair to pitch.

I slip it on and lure my lover
to the Perseids. Slide under
the fence. Current pulses
where cicada whir in the orchard.
Five heifers chew out the night air
and sigh like farm women.

We toss my late Dad's overcoat
across uneven pasture grass and our
selves upon it till her silk threads
ravel under his fingers: seam by dart
weft from warp and meteors
pelt down like easy silver.

O moon
release my mother from insomnia.
Let the bridegroom enter.
Claim her in the tomb-deep
rolling calm.

O, MA

Evenings you
Leaned into the mirror,
Mouth, intent over teeth:
An O. Upper lip, the curve,
Halfhearted as valentines
We snipped, symmetrical,
At school.

Each red sweep
Said, "Here's how to be
A lady."

This morning
Our mortician says
You are not ready.

"Well, that's okay."
He unzips the corduroy sack,
So like a baby carrier.
Your mouth, an O,
Tense over teeth.
I toss my heart in. Look!
It fits.

2.

SUDDEN EDEN

1968: A MOTHER RELATES

Why she would trade in
her birthright for a hill of beans
escapes me!

Ten or twelve of them plunked down their life
savings, Israel Bonds, anything they could lay
their hands on for a hovel and a hundred acres
of calluses a widow was singing and dancing to
put behind her.

My daughter cut up her presentable clothes
and braided the strips into area rugs.
"It's drafty. Why doll yourself up to slop
the hogs?" Farming reminds her of Mother
Russia, her roots.

So who wants to remember digging for skimpy
potatoes among strangers who will never have you
over, even for a drink of water?
My daughter writes,
"The wind teaches us humility."

I rest my case!

INVOCATION

Night fits down a tight lid
over our valley, cauldron-deep.
We gather kindling to earn our sleep.

God help us, refugees in winter-dress
Skating home on thin ice
from the Apocalypse.

BLUE SEAL

Did you ever fall open
like a hundred-weight
of Blue Seal Dairy Ration?

Release to the pull
of the sack trick string and let
all your particles spill into tin?

       Through our skewed barn door
       Dawn unscrolled seasons
       across Bessie's drafty stall.

       I pressed my brow against her dark flank,
       centered the scalded pail below
       her clean worn teats.

Did you ever surrender to
hunger and have your fill of that
sweet loved feed?

       She sniffed, shifted about, lifted her head
       for the slow chew. Licked with a rough
       elastic tongue. Swallowed. Allowed her

four stomachs with the names of Biblical kings,
Rumen, Omassum, Abomassum, Reticulum,
to do as they were meant.

Your hands get the hang of their task.
Life falls into place.
Frothy, warm, fluent

from all quarters
it gushes, ricochets
and pools.

SUDDEN EDEN

For that pinkish haze across the orchard,
ten thousand blossoms on a widow's peak,

we forsook The Revolution
and bought the farm.

He bought the farm means *kicked the bucket,*
croaks Maynard, our helpful neighbor, who *did*

decades later, never owning
what he woke to milk.

September 15th, the sun, a blanched peach,
our possession. In the kitchen,

I have heard the mermaids singing,
Hale and Elberta, Hallelujah.

The wood stove hums Home Comfort.
Cool, pare, halve, stone.

Leave half-an-inch of head space,
tips the manual.

We slip
our hearts

into wide-mouth
winter.

JANUARY COUNTER

What is not white between us
is this hyacinth erupting
from a chilled bulb

which you, though skeptical,
have nested in pebbles.

What is not white is somewhere
between the bruise of dusk
and the periwinkle of
my flannel dress.

Before the stove dims
I am watching
what is white fail
while the blues flare from
an improvised vase.

The hyacinth consumes itself.
White roots clasp the stones
and take trace minerals
as the old bulb blows.

Not yours, Joan.
Your blue flame holds
and feeds from what
unnamable tuber?

CHANCE MEETING

My neighbor swears
this spring might finish him.

Beside the mailboxes
hunched and clustered

like a trailer park
we pause to speak.

Damp hay, late corn, low yields,
the listing barn, his son's not into it.

"How's the poetry going?"
he politely asks.

"About like my jalopy....
Cheaper than livestock."

"No feed bills," he quips. "Well,
you just can't count on ends to meet..."

The scenic field across the road
he'll cut for cash.

Our sentences tail off like cow paths
in juniper once the herd's been sold.

"Hyah..." His low indrawn sigh
like the stroke of a scythe.

FIRST CUTTING

From the feel it must have been nearly
noon when she appeared. The farmer
who refused a hat adjusted the cutterbar
lower for the stoneless field. Over his
shoulder, the swath of timothy could've

collapsed from heat alone. The foreign
woman (polka-dot shirt and slacks) lost
her hat executing cartwheels through his
windrows. Her body spaced apart like
spokes: a perfect arc the fresh bale cut

from kicker to cart. He called, "Grab
that straw hat or I'll bale it!" She shouldn't
be here like the whip of birch he'd left
to grow. Interfered with his mower. Was
no longer silver. Still he liked the motley

shade. She strode beside the tractor and
insisted above the din: daisies bled and black-
eyed Susans winced before the scissoring.
More than once he paused as she untwisted
tendrils of purple vetch and wound them

around his neck: a feather boa. He showed her
a tortoise shell the size of a soup tureen; a spot
at the stubble edge where a red fox stalked free
lunch; the glen where hummingbirds nursed in
irises his mother had flung from her cluttered

garden. He cautioned, "Wear shoes." She showed
her bare foot to his open palm: tough, accustomed
to ill-use. She followed the tractor down to the
distant house where he mangled her name for his
mother, neighbor, sister, son and wife.

FLIGHT SONG

Even the comic strips
are topical:
Mutt and Jeff coerce
a recalcitrant cow.

I climb from barn to house
with milk and wonder
what makes that woman step on her own tit?
(Our children visit their fathers.)

Making no headway with this inquiry,
I rinse my daughter's undies in the sink
although the well is low
and let the wind inflate the leg holes.

Just then the geese cross
with their rusty cry of reeled in wash--
the effort that it takes to keep
from flight.

My heart is turned out like
a pocket: lint, pen, paper clip,
a little change. Prudent,
I pin it to the line.

Suddenly the hills are bleachers.
With their pompoms
the trees spell out
Resist Migration.

FRUITING BODIES

Weary of the garden
I prop the hoe
and wander.

Under a landmark oak
a drift of chanterelles
juts from moss.

Chanterelle--
let my tongue
tangle in your names:

Oreja de liebre: hare's ear,
Rehfüsshen: deer's foot,
Vaqueta: small cow,

Dooierzwam: egg yolk,
Mãozinhas: baby hands,
Rebozuelo, woman's dress,

Rubito: little blond,
Vingesvamp: wing fungus,
Xochilnanácatl: flower.

Ah, the fruiting body of
desire! Chanterelle: a trill
of thrush made edible.

LAW OF FALLING BODIES

Gravity draws equally on light
and heavy falls.

Syncopating wind: the Baldwins
patter among the Merinos who
nose them, chomp and ruminate.

We mosey through the orchard
sampling the crop. Late fruit
keep its edge as frost

fleeces the pasture. The ewes
are easy. Soon the ram will
coax them, hooves on flanks,

filling their girth with singletons,
twins, triplets to dive down
in a driving blizzard, slide out

or be midwifed, thrive or totter,
huddle by the south wall,
lolling in winter sun.

Eight apples for a pie.
And one for the plump lamb,
a flawless drop.

Sizing up her side
I map our chops.

NEIGHBORS

Only one way to stay friends forever:
Keep your shoulder to the wheel or out of view.
You crack weak jokes and laugh about the weather

wearing you down to bank loans, sweat and leather.
Kitchen heat's a halo we stare through.
Only way to stay just friends forever

is for me to sterilize these mason jars
and boil the season's surplus into stew.
Weak glass cracks from shock in changing weather.

My wrist inside your hand feels like a feather
falling from me. Your arms will not pursue
the only way to stay. Friends forever

give and take their wrenches, sugar, spreaders.
If favors ask too much and debts accrue,
they crack weak jokes and wonder, wonder whether

it's worth it. Screen door slams. Fan blades blur
my husband's face. His half-wave hails and warns you:
"Stay to dinner friend and starve forever."
Weak men crack like trees in frigid weather.

FOR OUR ROAD COMMISSIONER ON RETIREMENT

How often sleeper wake to the distant din
And sudden, slow approaching light. The plow
Roars through our dreams and tucks us in again.
Visions of the night world dance with snow-
Enchanted boughs and wind-invented drifts.
You engineer each answer to the season's
Liquid challenges and gaping rifts,
Calling for laughter mixed with vigilance.
Universal quirks and qualms respond
To jokes as well as levelheadedness.
The roads you smooth and tend bear us beyond
Impasses. On roads ripped from the wilderness
Neighbors swerve and weave their lives together,
Give or take the tension of the weather.

OVERALL

1.

Sun on frost:
ice flowers the fire
pond.

Summit:
odd cries cross hills
I count

sixty snow geese
two strict Vs
undersides silver

winging against the
current outer towing
the weaker.

Ten pull away from
the hard row and hover
in plowed air.

2.

Quilts on the yard
pillow of bedrock
by the luck

of the almanac
I lie under
the Leonids.
domesticating night.
Black enamel
speckled sky...

Old canner. Ball jar
meteors spew shards
and fruit.

It is nothing
like
this.

DECADES AND ACRES IN STRIDE

That antique mare
lets her folk song hair hang down
like water over the dam.

Your muddy ridge road we amble,
land-poor, ravenous to tell who
fell for   kicked out
took in   blew through
stuck by   saw to

Decades lumber
under barn boots.

Your parsnip soup,
uprooted from a raised bed,
simmers on a trivet.

My pie, the Northern Spies, thaws.
Each fruit, a face
pulled from November snow.

So we grew, on twin mountains,
tons for vegetable-scorning
kith or kin. How come?

56

Wind in the chimney
coos…

Maples lace us
to uncertain skies.

Sap soon.

IN WILD STRAWBERRIES

June.... the red scent.
two young men I know
hunt

frais du bois
savoring the foreign
tongue.

Heart-seed berry
(the Narragansett
named it)

thriving
in a habitat
for serpents.

Up the acid pasture
they bend crawl sample
share *fragaria*.

One palm paints
the other.
Sun consents.

DESIRE IN A SPRING SQUALL

So (goes the snow)
Let silver
edges

     mesh
     embed
     enfold!

Limbs
double
in bulk.

     Lie down
     in a
     pasture

thicker
than
thieves.

     O snow
     you make me
     want to.

SERENADE

You have not awakened to cicada
and opened the side door
to hear their queer radar
or the frogs pulling the plug
in the beaver pond below.

Fog before morning
moves her. Unfinished sleep is
a night dress not warm enough.
The house turns over.

She steps away to touch
her vegetables whose colors wave,
to crush a beetle, sample a leaf,
to sense the fresh growth
curving and red
to the full moon
September,
and before completion
she bends to them.

Spread your back against the planet.
Soon, soon enough we are sealed
and shelved like pitted fruit emitting

a gold or greenish flickering glow
like fireflies in a jar with a punctured lid,
and soon forgotten as the science
of a child's midsummer night,
up late collecting.

Rest before frost. Rest because
the clouds (which are trout or wishes
or couches) tomorrow may be oracles.
Unroll the way a bucket tossed
in a well is slowly filled.

See how in ripeness
the peach
detaches.

NOCTURNE

Sleeper, wake unalarmed in a garden
scented with nicotiana or snow.
Rise in the heart of night
not to cool a fever
or temper a dream.
The moon
wants company.
She tosses her shawl
on your quilt.
The bridegroom
(should there be one)
barely stirs.

The pillow will level
the valley you leave.
See the luna moth
drawn on your screen,
her kite of metamorphic silk.
Consider the teakettle-sheen
of the stars.

Through the needle-eye
of nightfall, ancestors
pierce trees and stones,
easing home
as you will.

Here is the skein.
Unravel.
Return.

3.

FIRESTONE

FIRESTONE

1.

Memory insists
like buttons on a mattress
that trained our sleep
into a slalom course:
there were two ways to lie down
without harm and I remember them.

2.

So few cars drove over our dirt
you could read their tread—
rickrack, meander like the trim
of an urn.

By noon the sun leveled
the mud so soft on the road bed
you couldn't leave driving.

3.

I kept open to you
like a culvert (strong ribbed silver)
a conduit for torrents, so that your fits
and starts relenting wouldn't wreck us.
You didn't have to ask: it was instinct

4.

That year the *Times* had a great spread
on the pterosaur: its wingspan so wide
they wondered how it flew.
Someone sent us a post card
of a stone sarcophagus for two
from the Met—*Always together
just like you.*

Since no one will dig up imprints
of our fossil claws, I'll scratch
an epitaph out of all possible language.

Side by side we made the best of
seven years' dark luck: a passionate,
monumental mismatch.

Eyes mum from dissembling.
Lips sculpted into manic smiles.

SIX PAST EIGHT A.M., AUGUST 13TH

At nine her car will roll you
Into a ball. So enter and discuss
The ramifications of a kiss....

Our trees display their seven greens.
Beyond these filmy windows
I watch the diorama of ripeness
Seeking its own decay.

A hawk stretches and flashes
The white underside of his wings
In a royal flush.

Around this chair the cats are hunting
Dust. I am at one the with the kitchen clock
Gritting its tiny teeth, telling the truth,
The icebox which is kind
Of a window when one is no longer
Hungry, the houseflies abuzz on the ceiling.

Who of us is not out for blood?
Under the awning of seven greens
She wants to be moist and honest.

What do you do with a woman
Whose warm arms
Imply that this is possible?

I am a grounding rod.
I am the surest path for lightning.

Give it to me or the house will burn.

TROUBLE TIME

An old nurse's trick from *Troubled Times*—

In a pinch, mix Milk of Magnesia
with white table sugar.
Spread on the sore to build a scar.

Blue window, sugar snow.
Moonlight coats the glass
like Milk of Magnesia...
The grid of winter is
over our bed.

One red line...
the inside of his eyelid
vigilant in sleep.

His arm
across my back
a strap, a question mark.

Motion
seconded by the clock.

Stillness, the salve
of privacy on my skin,
I trace a spell
across the pillowslip.

Let *I* be *she*.

O soothe, sooth, soot.
Subtract me.

OPEN SEASON

A man is fishing beside a final shelf of snow.
In retreat, the white is more like shell fungus on
a rotted beech not the sea it was.

He casts and dips next to rocks, logs, deeps
and overhangs even as his sneakers sink and fill.
There is no suddenness until infant trout bite,
rise and commence to suffocate. Six
in quick succession he unhooks and splashes
back to life. They flash away.

Late April rain, for seconds. Where beavers
have rerouted their waterworks this spring,
he stops to smoke. Evening light tents the man,
his red shirt, blue hat. Soon, he will head back,
offer her his catch and watch her next move...

The woman squatting on the other bank is
someone else's wife. She tries to lose
sight of this, observing about her boots,
skunk cabbage, salamanders, mushrooms
she can't name, *not the moment she'll spring*
from his Chevrolet, crushed leaves, coiled ferns
to the prior claim of another man and kin,

a web with rain, precarious in a forked twig;
bloodroot, trillium *she should have fins*.

She focuses on the primary blur of red and blue
pushing through brush without haste
the way a water strider stirs the pond,
flexing noiselessly across its face.

Later, she will not ask, "Does the hook hurt
no matter how deftly it's removed?" Or,
"How long can one live outside its element?"
She could lean on the car hood and joke
about cold feet, while he slits each fish and
shows the husks of bugs it had for lunch.

No, she will stroke the trout and marvel
at its silver resilience, its eagerness
to snatch the lure.

AMONG THE AWNINGS
Memorial Day

A lilac hedge on the Commons...
she broke the twigs. Said --Here,
darling. *Carpe diem*.

Scent juts like smoke
from the aqua canning jar.

> Even the street sweats under cars lunging
> with their contents toward some lunch—
> hot dogs, cold cuts, black flies, tag sales,
> tantrums, pony rides.

The landscape is her print
dress draped over his chair...

> Somewhere out of orbit...
> a child, man, lawsuit, food
> to purchase and to plant...

or his blue vein she traces
hip to knee with her fingernail.

Across the park: a bugle. Adoration
        of the graves, self-sacrifice.
        The fanned-out maple shades
        the steeple clock, its hands
        still legible in April.

        Flags and anthems end
        in the band-shell.

She ceases to keep track
except by bells.

PRIMA GRAVIDA

Wet a goblet. Rub the rim. Imperfection
sings. Run the faucet until water bellies.

Professor X praised surface tension years
ago as I dozed missing how matter bellies…

Ninth month. We wait, oafs on a sofa;
loaves and fishes in our tauter bellies.

I skim the *Geographic*: Wallaby stashes
joey in a pouch to flee from predator bellies.

Glossy poses: rage bulges from baggy
camouflage: behold, child-soldier-bellies.

Grin and spar: Re-enactors mock-make war.
Who volunteers for *Pieta, Gold Star* bellies?

Wind lends drama drapery for agony and bliss.
Wind groans or coos to mother-martyr bellies.

Perfection song: *Your turn to be round. Ring true,
Verandah. The tongue in this bell never lies.*

VILLANELLE IN APRIL

One night the beavers breached the dam and fled
Leaving a rutted crater in their wake.
Suddenly her water floods the bed.

Come out and hear the woodcocks court! he said.
How curious the ruckus that they make.
That night the beavers breached the dam and fled.

Two adolescent hawks wheeled overhead.
Later she sees their figure-eights in the dark
As suddenly her water floods the bed.

We've had more rain than we anticipated.
The weather hovered over tea and cake
The night the beavers breached the dam and fled.

It's somewhere between a rock and a loaf of bread:
She laughed. *But how much longer will it bake?*
Afterwards her water floods the bed.

He sang: *The antiseptic scent of melted
Snow. The season opens like an egg!*
That night the infant breached the dam and slid
From her. The beavers slapped their tails and fled.

SUMMER DUSK: OUR PRIMER

cushioned in green our grounds feel st**A**
ble possible. the daughters gab in ba**B**
talk & play whiffle ball so we **C**
they've **D**
cided to love **E**
ch other. nobody strikes out. l**F**
t to its own devices summer's this apolo**G**
a sudden bonus like a p**H**
eck so late it's windfall profit. **I**
fritter hours under **J**
blue skies. sun rolls a cro**K**
ball through a silver hoop smooth as **L**
la fitzgerald on the boom box. you **M**

pty out your day: **N**
tertain us with choice divorces. *the narrO*
fellow in the grass a **P**
vish banker elopes with the **Q**
pee doll whose ex was **R**
S
ted pushing snow. it's better than **T**
v while deadheading fairy roses. i'm un**U**
sed to evenings when swank hea**V**
musk of lilies makes bees see **W**
and i should have such luck: unearned **X**
travagance. love-in-a-mist! **Y**
can't we seal this? it looks so E-**Z**

KITCHEN HINTS: NOT TO ENTER
WINTER EMPTY-HANDED

1.

Hold a candle to a mirror.
Spell out the lover's name in tallow.
Dip a spatula in water.
If brittle letter-blobs chilled on silver
won't lift off evenly
set him aside.

2.

Fill a black sky-speckled kettle
with a rolling boil.
Steam quart jars.
Can light.
Seal and cool.

3.

Take a cleaver to red cabbage.
Thunk! Choose half.
Ink its imprint: dense violet strata
curved around a geologic core.
Pull yourself together.
Shred the clean side
for a tart slaw. Serve.

4.

Root for your future.
Bring daughters into wind.
Bend to the field.
Watch their white hands
numb and gladden
around red potatoes.

Say: Dig for our ancestors.
See with your fingers.
Quick work.
Frost's no false alarm.

5.

Squash song
Simmer forever my delicata:
two-toned thick-skinned winter keeper.
Why take a lifetime to be tender?
Beside you the slick seeds burn.

NIGHT PORTRAIT

Ten below
the trees play air
guitar; the house rocks.
Ten miles from anyone
on her wavelength
Daughter stretches
thirteen years across
the freezer chest and tells
the red telephone to
touch someone.

Beneath her
summer rests in its own
ice age: plastic bags of
cauliflower, sausage
from the last sow.
There's no rush
to pry loose this produce.
She can nest
against laundry
and pen rock lyrics on her
best-worn jeans.
Only the ancient washer
flips its lid.

Mom's catatonic on the sofa;
stepdad's feeding fires with
forests; kid sister pesters her
within an inch
of violence.

No warmth counts
but what wires bear
from lip to ear
when loneliness is
sleet.

FEB

1.

Oxymorons Set Their Taps

 Squalid wealth! Splendid filth
of the first melt!

2.

Tan-scape Chant

Cattail goldenrod sword grass mud.
Leaf mold clapboard dog food wood.
Chevrolet dead with a dented hood.
Jersey heifer chewing her cud.
Pitchfork frozen in the pockmarked sod.
Shell-shocked neighbor walking to God.

3.

A Toy O Toyota

Today has blizzard written all over it
like the snow leopard, spots under fur.

This silver car   (the salesman swore)
can split the drifts the clouds fling down.
She sprawls on their bed. Can't wait
for the worst   laughing.

4.

Snow Day

Wheels whir. Studs glide like slurred speech.
Streets slick as they come...
between Wash and Linc
she takes him in
her legal legs.

ICE OUTAGE

Over the hump
of a storm
dumb luck
kicks in

No land line
ring tone
Our *say*
stays put

Search
engine
the private
eye

cardinal intent
on suet

Night fall
lamp chimney
so like a
torso

Oil and wick
flame sips.

As ice to twig
we click.
Snug fit.

TWO SKIES WAILING HOME

1. 4 A.M. 1973

Sobs erupt like bubbles in pabulum.
From unfathomable slumber
I surface serviceable as a spoon.
He tumbles back to bed
with a sack of broken sleep.
Our breath plumes.

Cunning mammal girl
she roots to me as dawn
waters down the puffed stars'
dry formula.

2. 10 P.M. 1988

Ike and Tina wail *Rolling on the River*
 "easy first then rough" like ten
asphalt-to-dirt miles to the sticks.

Daughter says (as she always does)
"Ike's a dog but any woman could
fall all over his bass line."

From the mouths of babes...
too soon.

Just then *Aurora borealis*
blues the windshield
like nothing
more than liquid
miracle detergent.

MARCH WITH HER BLUES

Jack *did* Dawn (swore not to) now no call,
No idling in the drive. My daughter can't
draw around her blazing psyche the blank
she wants more than a Marlboro Light.
His ream of un-spelled poems she tears
in bite-sized lies to please the fire.

Faithful friends drive over for a bonfire.
Barbecue some brush & furniture; she calls
it pagan pyromania. Lush flames tear
into the scrap heap. That hiss, an incantation
over saplings, studs & drawers. "Light
of my life," she sneers & pitches his blanket,

unsettling the pheromones, dna, drab, lank
hair, late cigarettes, the wool on fire.
State by state, she shreds the atlas; recalls
the dream-trips, traced on blue veins. "Can't
go there." March in the frigid mud. Time tears

at the calendar. She hibernates between tiers
of wash, fiction, orange peels, old "blankitty,"
her pet security rag, shells & curios she can't
jettison. Jim Morrison wails "Light My Fire,"

a warped LP, a motion picture mating call
that straddles time. Strike anywhere: she lights

a stick of sandalwood, a candle, Camel Light.
Little Anthony and the Imperials chant "Tears
on My Pillow." "Love is not a gadget," calls
me back from one bad pastime: drawing a blank
on the gaping screen. I feed the kitchen fire,
half-forgotten, and her face. Sorry I can't

come back with a catchy duet or descant.
Pie bakes. Root soup simmers on the pilot light.
I pat the sofa. Leave the stove ajar, see the fire:
Yeats' "glowing bars," the sparks, a crown of tears.
Dickinson says, "Pain has an element of blank."
Who needs oblivion? Heartache is a close call.

Remember how you call the mare & canter
across blank pastures or when northern lights
flare over us like paper roses tearing into fire.

MY TURN TO EXFOLIATE

My girl I bet your lucky skin has nothing
to bitch about. Your blush like a nectarine.
You can leave behind the Pilotonic Placenta
Body Shop cruelty-free potions
and lack nothing.

Near empty upside-down I utilize your beauty
secrets: *In an upward motion avoiding eyes*
I lightly apply the last of an Alpha-Hydroxy
Peel-off Masque. Its Sugar Cane and Guava
clear and jellied slick on stick to me and shine.

While my face shrinks I size up your ex-room.
See how cells sloughed and flung like Victoria's
Secret lingerie have fluffed into beautiful dust-
tufts and boas: the five o'clock shadow
of July and August. I box what now

you'd never be caught dead in while it's easy
to do without you. Beyond this view the pink
rose you planted dopes the Japanese beetles.
They burrow and wallow like those cads
from Vernon. I crush them

and save face peeling off this
second skin like the sunburn
we can't stop shredding
though we know it
scars.

DAUGHTER AND WATERFOWL

1.

Baby weighs me down
like a gallon of milk.
Through swamp and thicket we hike
to the heronry: woody nests
set in crotched boughs.

Great blues swoop from
the canopy. Chicks gape suck air
keen for chewed blood.

.

Cloud over water: good light
for winged foragers. One crested
omnivore with a Jurassic cry
could pluck her from me.
I clap him back.

2.

Not her first beau just the hottest
Adam. No home to speak of. Lost boy
on rusty stunt bike he steadies her
on handlebars and flies
through the Chopper lot

dodging cop strobes
shopping carts. Laughter
in the neon dark.

Her hair unpins and floods
his shoulders. Does she put on his
knowledge with his power?
Sure as his prize hooded fleece
slips over her spine.

VALENTINE

Rescuing the china chips from trash

I watch you piece a goblet back to use:

Cement its crooked joints so any smash

Holds history as well as wine, reviews

A fumble to anticipate a toast.

Restless in this bed, I watch late clouds

Drift apart like marriages and coast,

Converging only when the wind allows.

Out where love won't keep a cloud intact,

Unhindered by the mind, you cross the sheets

To fix my body with a single fact:

Allegories crumple, obsolete.

No metaphor of crockery and glue

Takes after how I've filled and empty you.

NOTICE

Girl you slip on your step-
grand-wedding tux your father-ex-
lover-red stilettos my late-dad-
neck-ware kid-sister-mardi-gras-love-
beads my-shawl-belt-turban...
Wearing us all out
you sprint through dazzle-
drifts to catch the wave some
rays your ride a cold
your shadow I'm still
rapping on the window
Don't trip!

CHECKING BACK INTO THE DRIFTWOOD

Bailey Island, ME

We can't curtail the desk clerk's chat.
Her white permanent, a still life of surf.

I break away. You follow.
It's decades since we landed here,

October newlyweds, elated under ear flaps
and overcoats puffed with vows.

"Try our chowder," the waitress recommends.
"It has nondairy creamer now."

We pass. She lists the dressings.
Odd, what advice we memorize or lose.

At what coastal point had someone lettered
across a boulder's thigh--

CAUTION: the waves
are of uneven size?

*

Nothing more pressing now
than skin and scavenge.

Twice a day the sea disrobes
rocks, knocks metaphors

off the bureau.
Lobstermen in rubber ware

bob home...their skiff love-names
half-visible in the chop.

My book:
Rachel Carson with a hand lens

magnifies and muses.
We belong among mosses.

Nightfall our single bed
hard by the sound--

Speech! speech!
backslapping gulls beseech...

Unscramble
our nimble conundrum...

Transliterate
the tide.

4.

POET IN RESIDENCE

LIES ABOUT EXCELLENCE

Two-room elementary school

1.

Rob imagines--

> I love riding in the
> fields with me and my
> Dad side by side. Dad
> says *Hey I'll beat you*
> *to the house* so I
> gallop through the windy
> brown grass. I feel great
> riding by my Dad as he
> laughs like Santa
> flying in the wind!

2.

Rob says his cat Spot caught a cute chickadee.
Dad cried, "Cut it out!" and pitched a sharp stick
hard at bad Spot, catching Rob's lid not an inch

above his eye. The raw scar's right there, see?
Dad didn't want to hurt, and like
the cat, could not do otherwise.

3.

Rob's sharp as stings, as hard to ease.
He dreams all over his desk. The day he tries to
choke himself in class, kids gasp and snicker.
A future Eagle Scout invents the harshest crack.
The teacher comes to Rob with calm. He cries,
"Why hold it in for hours? All you can get
for doing good is stickers."

4.

They get
seven hours central heat, tap water,
scrubbed johns, free peanut butter,
shelves of toys, facts rolled up, ready
to show themselves; maps of everywhere
beyond this two-room town.
Three women pull the maps down
to pronounce the names kids need
to leave here, or to stay on

103

their fathers' upturned plots, hawking
"the Taste of Vermont":
some legal yuppie crop with a joke name
like *shiitake* mushrooms.

5.

It's so fine this afternoon,
the whole school's out on the wheelchair ramp
with paper and pencils praising the sun.

The big kids act so proud
to have apologized.
Even the girls shake loose
their public voices for this thaw.

Jeremiah, second grader, whispers:

> The wrmth is odd
> becus it is stil wintr
> but I lik it.
> I fel esy on myslef,
> rel esy on myslef.

WRITE FOR YOUR LIFE!

Four bongs.
> The steeple bells set ten young Bics
> to jitter or glide.

Words are cheap! cheap! cheap!
> jeer the squirrel-birds bobbling
> through teenage oaks.

I've picked your name to praise
> brunette waves silver stud
> eyes below shades India skirt and upturned arch.

You have explained the poverty of love—
> four lame rhymes in the father tongue
> and the hairpin turn from knit to ravel
> kiss to shove.

Tears can't organize a stanza
> so the sun gilds those tiny mirrors
> sewn to the hem of your poem.

DEATH'S KID BROTHER

regional high school

"Keg weather": the Full Flower Moon
has use for human sacrifice, so some
senior boy without credit to graduate
drowns. As I blow into school, girls
are chipping in on American Beauty
roses to toss over the falls
he took their hearts down:
white water, head of foam,
the margins of his yearbook snapshot.
Petals separate like polished nails.

Serene among the weeping blonds,
this drowned boy's brother
impish Dracula, prowls the corridors
cloaked in the crow-winged overcoat
he just inherited. Death wreathes
his spiked hair in a crown of thorns.

Write for me. It's time.
I tell the live boy.
Remember what a pest I am,
he boasts.

In sloppy script, all loopholes and tight angles,
the kid brother knocks this out:

The stares in the night sky

look like their about to burst and

the apple blosoms on the apple trees

look like their about to burst but

the best of all is when pretty girls

passing by in cars wave their hands at me then

I feel like I'm about to burst.

Back home I start hanging out my wash.
The black phone rings indoors.
Clouds for a hundred tons of storm
roll over. How many drops will score?

I think everyone flirts with
Death's kid brother. I single out his
work and pull down damp shirts singing:

Life's not done for
till there's no more dirt.

One red tongue-tied sock's
still pinned to my taut line
by the time it pours.

THERESA, 13, TELLS HOW

Make your mind blank out
I'm like you fool
Around with the dials and the
Program twists into ribbons
No faces just weird shapes
Like shadows the bedroom
Blinds make some nights
On the ceiling.

You switch off
And the show shrinks down
To a peephole a pinprick
Then nothing

So not matter who tries
To sell what to whom
It all goes into the dark
I start making before

The hall light pull-cord
Swings free so by the time
He's near my shoulder with his
Slow-motion whispering
Hands I'm tuned out
As good as gone.

You know you don't
Get marks for it

You have to teach yourself
From scratch.

PERSEPHONE ELOPES

Watch her steps
on any ancient frieze:

He's a terrorist; she's his
mission: the country he'll kill
for. He says he'll blow apart
her home if she doesn't come
now shielding him and
she does beautifully—

The girl as cigarette
igniting when he draws
on her. Feline: nine lives
spoken for.

He is her fiancé.
His stolen gold in her bedroom
she alone can handle.

She likes his foreign taunt:
"I claim responsibility."

Don't ask. She won't snap
out of it or straddle
his shadow.
He wants to take her
underground.

MACHINING THEIR STORY

Mel straightened the recliner to open our interview--

We had lost our father. My mother was supporting three boys as a weaver.
Then the mill closed down. We were up against it.

    Folks in this lack-luck town knew how to yank
    themselves back to work. They called it, "Yankee   ingenuity."

    Boys banked on stamina, Scout's honor: peddled news,
    popcorn; killed fowl, split and hauled bucks, forests;
    shored up sills and siblings; camped on the precipice;
    hands hankered to tinker, minds to fine-tune steel.

    Daughters came to grips with an ax, mop, skillet, needle
    or mangle; infants fell into place; formula warmed before
    dads did. Third shift she ran wool or rayon. Hooked shades
    with *Praying Hands*, tuned up the Arctic Cat, the Firebird.

There was always that tenseness about not having enough.
Just a fact of life: we never went hungry.

        I type and weep. Blind Justice, peel your eyes!
        Is Childhood none of your business?

Don't make us sound so noble and somber.

      Correct. Delete.

Remember after work we drove down to Roseland
and danced like fools to bands you couldn't dream of.

      Stick a spigot in granite.
      Life is sweet.

SEPTEMBER AT "THE HOME"

Her hands still farm the sheets.
When years outweigh the body, I perch
by her bed and whisper, *Speak to me.*
Chrome catches the diamond ring that

hangs from her finger as a good dress
would from the rack of her spine.
By God (she swears) *You'd better
believe.* We fill the larder, pare

core and quarter hours, scare up jars
of relishes and jams, mince, quince.
Lestoil douses cinnamon. We talk down
dim stairs where a new screw-in electric

bulb shaped like a summer squash sheds
light on all she's squared away. We slip
tomatoes from their skins easier than
children, shuck and strip cobs' milk-

sweet, sticky silk. We tackle pickles:
bread & butters in pints, dills in brine
kept crisp with grape leaves, cool in the
crock held down by a plate and rock.

114

You have no idea how much we had!
she cries. Harvest holds us in place.
Our laps heap, famous
with all we have named.

100 YEARS OF SQUARES AND REELS

Winter nights your father filled the sleigh
with hay and drew the family toward

the music he didn't care to dance to.
You glided over rolled snow to the hill-town

Grange Halls where a fiddler and piano player,
fortified with a serious supper of oyster stew,

tossed off their repertoire of squares and reels.
Your red dress flounced, and fine young men

who took your hand could be counted on not to drink.
Like your mother before, you danced every figure

till the Morning Star was a warning. Come dawn,
the cow breath rose like question marks.

Still in the red dress stitched by the seamstress,
hemmed with straw and snow, you skipped over

the gutter and drew down the milk
before dreaming.

HER SORROW

Edwin my brother he just went down
Our older brother had a car with a rumble seat
He drove us to the lake that very day
We were singing all the way there

Our older brother had a car with a rumble seat
winding through the dust
we were singing all the way there
That's him on the wall

Winding through the dust
he was smaller than the others and not in their category
That's him on the wall
we were two little afterthoughts

smaller than the others and not in their category
I watched the water close
we were too little: Afterthoughts...
The Lord gave us to each other

I watched the water close
What drove us to the lake that very day
the Lord gave us one another?
Edwin my brother he just went down.

5.

OUR FALL

NANA GOES DADA: TOTAL LOSS FARM

Here on Easy Street I can compost the past.

Watch Oona's three pet pigmy goats
ransack the 60s: mildewed college texts
and the spidery library that housed them.

The goats, they're so damn cute:
dashing eyes, prim grins and party shoes.
Their horns storm the high shelves

and shucked selves tumble. An avalanche
of language litters the broadloom
and the goats consume.

I bend among burdocks
to brush and flatten page scraps.
The Age of Jackson blows into

Easy Blues Guitar. Gormenghast seeks
Deliverance.

> *...He was infatuated with all that pertained
> to love. He trod breast-deep through banks
> of thorn-crazed roses,*

Peake gushes. Dickey cleans his clock.

Beethoven's Clavier Sonata,

clefts and rests, is too far gone to play.
Wind harps on chicken wire.

A Tale of Two Cities tatters.
It is a far, far better patch of tarpaper
tacked to a scroll of polyethylene.

The New Golden Bough waves its muddy,
mythic leaves and *The Sun Also Rises*
on *General Chemistry*:

> *Justify from your own experience,*
> *the hypothesis that the vapor pressure*
> *of mercury is less than that of water...*

under the bridge. We mince words.
When the goats, sated with print,
tear my daffodils' frilled throats,

magnetic *morning* slips from
the fridge. I lure them back
with Stoned Wheat Thins.

O Spring during the white truce
of bloodroot nothing is meant
to sting.

PARASITES

I liked it better here before they came.
Sixteen years, I still don't know their names
Or what they do up there where Spence defied
The earth to make a crop before he died
Of anything worth marketing. His junk,
A field of faded, rusty cars and trucks
Was all he bothered with. His daughter tended
The house and land with a vengeance. She pretended
For the old man's sake and ours, to ask advice
Before she sowed or settled on the price
For so much as a pin.

              When his heart went bad
On him, she kept him home. He was all she had
For family ties. When he wouldn't swallow
Medicine, and waited, pale and sallow,
For the end, we wondered how long *after*
She would wait to wed. She needn't wear her
Grief for us, I thought. She lost her youth
Already to the father and that north-
Faced, windblown farm. Some decent widower
Might make a go of it with her. A wrecker
Could clear the fields in under a week. A coat

Of paint and kitchen curtains can do lots
To liven up a place and exorcise
Its ghosts.

        I'd be the last to criticize
Her, thwarted as she was up there, but when
She buried him, the dirt kicked up again.
You cannot read into another's heart,
Living or dead. Some said she outsmarted
All the neighbors with a tasteless joke.
To sell the father's farm like that bespoke
A seething grudge like biting the hand that fed
Her. How could she have hidden such bad blood
Beneath the face of work and sacrifice?

The week the hippie kids moved in the place,
All eight or 12 of them, no one was sure,
They painted *PARADISE* above the door
Where Spencer raved and shouted at the stars
While hauling broken motors up the stairs,
And no one dared to ask them if they meant
To mock or celebrate a life misspent.

MOONLIGHTING

"Where are we?"
"Somewhere in the Bronx. Don't ask."
Our cloak-and-dagger act's a parody of
"Girl in Trouble Saved by Man in Mask!"
I call to witness Silence, Charity, Submit, Desire,
women scored in slate, who stomached
centuries of gripe or dread.
I'd fled this city on a whim:
to cultivate a garden, turn a hand to odes.
Instead I cross this sea-green waiting room
where sirens, women cheated out of beauty,
shriek and keen against the blinds my fixer runs
his finger down, to dust. The window
streaks my face with strobes.
The river crawls like skin.
"I should charge you double, this is twins…

I'm moonlighting," sighs my abortionist,
his sacrifice to keep the kids in school. "Parochial,
high class," as if I'd miss what he was driving at
with flaming tools. "D & C's are murderous."
A wince. "Six hundred bucks or it's not practical."
And I have five: my nest egg plus a loan,

since "five bills" was the figure when he called
to name the code word, "'Endometriosis,'
my receptionist knows what it means."

I'm 22; the word means "this is the end.
O, empty me. Do your routine."
"Anesthesia's extra."
This is '68.
He makes a killing at the going rate.

VERMONT SKY '72

Why settle here and stay
Anonymous under the self-same
Sky? Does this sky, custom-made to fit
Between industrious, accusing fingers
And adjacent acres keep us strangers?
The clouds shuffle, cut and deal

Such seasons. Everyone deals
With them or splits. *Go or stay*;
Raise chalets, corn or stranger
Crops. Ha, ha. It's all the same
On private property. Wind fingers
The fields feeling what wealth will fit

Within a single summer: profit
Or loss. Weather-wise no kid deals
Out a crazier hand. What shrewd fingers
And suggestive gestures make us stay
Rooted like rock maples in the same
Stance for decades, and still strangers?

Since settling for stranger
Sights than cities the sky's come to fit
Me better, in much the same

Manner as my other half. What deals
We strike. I say, *You talk. I'll stay
And take it down.* My fingers

Typecast clouds not men: finger-
painted, mop-streaked, Santa-stranger.
I ache to mingle with the ones who stay
Away from us and trust we'll never fit.
I study weather metaphors, idealizing
Terse, wry cadences. Alas, the same

Elastic blue can't stretch us. The same
Sun's radiating hand narrows, points a finger,
Yet cannot bless. No sweet deals
Ease our game. A host of baffled strangers
Keeps claiming turf where only forest fits,
Where cutting back is the only way to stay

Clear. The same sky sculpts lovelier, stranger
Realms than my fingers can farm or fit
Into phrases that mean, *Deal me in. I'll stay.*

NEIGHBORS SWING BY

1.

Redneck-hick boys lounge and barrel around
three counties killing off six packs, school hours:
birds and stones. Up this driveway: no game

just the old commune. Decades since the widow
sold, those people never ask or offer but are okay
once you get used to how their dogs run loose

and women wear the pants; in summer not much more.
They weed bare-chested; act pissed when you peek.
Their home improvements look like shipwrecks.

2.

She squints through mist. November: hunters, neighbors.
Even the clouds around them look like Wonder Bread.
Rifles poke from the truck bed: not much action yet.

She wants to know how to eat from these woods. Not
the blast of weighing in public what you've mastered.
Just to lay in a winter's safe free meat, herself (Okay,

scoff!). It's hard to shoot what nurses on your shirt.
She wonders why only the men come by. Their patriarch
always questions, half-cocked, "Who's in charge here?"

3.

One late July the neighbor, silver-haired and shy,
swings by with his latest lady who read the party sign
on the old apple tree. "Just passing through…"

 "No, No! Come eat. You're not intruding. Stay."
She fusses, hands them humus, grape leaves, pours…
Three vodkas smoother they salute their kids,

the rocky fields he hayed here for a buck a day.
"My folks have filled the bone-yard up the road
for centuries: Only time we sit still. Haw-haw."

"My people," she brags, "never went outdoors."
They toast the end of interloper-years,
their giddy stumble into bosom friendship.

He pats her hand. "Hey, you
kids taught me to respect what
I couldn't stand."

STOVEPIPE

She called, "We're leaving. Lay the fire at dusk; kindling's in
The corner box." Five of four: light bent down as if to milk.
"Open the door softly I've something to tell you, dear."
Varicose sky: a dark ache. I twisted yesterday's newsprint
Events so the headlines squinted, pitched them in the stove;
Pretty twig teepee, dry split ash; struck a match and poof.
In walked the children. Flame gleamed through the stove
Pipe thinned to lace. "It's okay," the boy says, "the fire,
Even so. The stovepipe. It's tender. Just a little tender."

COLD FIGURES ON THE HOLLOW
for Ron Squires

Dim days, thin light, shadowless:
we bundle up and try to throw our weight
around the pond. Wet blades press

for grace against rough ice.
Wind's hand-me-downs, we skate.
Days dim. Light thins, shadowless:

your breath, your pulse, precarious,
cornered by the chart. Straight
across the pond, wet blades press

the imprint of our helplessness.
Helterskelter jag-ruts recreate
dim days. Your skin is shadowless.

Once agile as a catamount, your prowess,
easy as luck, a line cast without bait
across the pond. Wet blades press

your date in stone. Without our blessing,
Death lays out the banquet, cleans your plate.
Day dims. Light thins. Shadowless
you cross. His wet blade lets you pass.

FOR RALPH AFTER GRIEF

1.

Your laughter, *Hyar, hyar!*
tore out of air the birds never heard
where I was raised, indoors.

Long ago when I was green
on the commune as the wood we burned,
you hitched snowshoes to my clumsy boots.
I waded by you onto the whiteness, my first
fishy steps against perfection, while you
reminisced about the Great Depression,
good years on the farm.

Chores done, you'd snowshoe overland
to the yard where deer sparred and ripped up
turnips planted on the hill for winter feed
and your amusement.

Does gossiped; bucks fought on their hind legs
crazy as men. You'd watch, gauge hunger,
maybe take one.

One summer I lost my bearings on that side hill,
overgrown with juniper and berries plump as I was,
pregnant with a second kid. I filled my mouth
with fat fruit so as not to weep and followed
deer tracks to the stream and home.
You'd shown me how.

2.

"Ma?" you roar.
I ask after her health at 88.

"She's like a boiled owl.
The more you cook it the tougher it gets."

3.

Now we'll cross paths each few months,
idle our motors to catch up:
both of us working counties far from our farms.

I skirt around the worst
 (your son is dead, was it a year?)
and joke until the backed up traffic balks.

"You come by soon! I'll call,"
and roll away.

TO HELL IN A HANDBASKET
for Andy Kopkind

Andy, cancer tears you away
from the neighborhood where your
summer chickens strut and feed
among potted orchids and the whole

hill is coming out from under
April. *Like a patient etherised*
upon the cruelest month, you quip.
You need someone to go to your root

cellar for the tender show bulbs
to spread among good friends' gardens.
Canna, calla, dahlia, glads.
Reach into the crypt, you laugh.

Below your kitchen, down steep stairs
I feel among heat ducts' hollow curves.
Things hang and seep, close
and moist: Is this what dark is like

within the body? --Remember unwrapping
The Sex Life of Flowers? Hummingbirds giving
head to bearded irises and monarchs
sucking milkweed. Andy, when the body

backfires blossoms stand in for all the
shapes a lover makes with us.-- I load
my wicker basket with your brown trousseau.
Look how each bulb or tuber fits
like a hand grenade about to blow.

WHAT COULD BE BAD

1. May Day

Fritz sets down a covered dish
for the pot luck.

"How've you been?"
He winces. "Positive."

2. Retro-Pioneer

Expelled from Ivy, Fritz hunkered
down in our adopted town to fake-farm.

Judge's son, he pumped hands, glad to
clear our path of what could be bad.

He studied cadences and gaits:
spoke and limp-strode like a dairy codger;

cruised town with "the boys," a yoke
of oxen too odd for the local Grange.

Fritz in love was a universal donor.
Straight-faced he posed to sundry women:

"Do you like bricks? I am digging clay."
His fair hair in August was a shock of wheat.
Surreptitious, plain as wind, his
innuendo spread, man to man…

This field holds the wealth of a bread basket.
Lie down. Consume. Come out.

3. Presidents Day

He has settled in a "painted lady"
with his mate, unwavering Tony.

Propped on the velvet sofa, he turns
to memorize the mountain and the town

he's passing through.
Tony calls him back —

"Darling try what I've brought you:
lime Jell-o with mandarin oranges."

Three gelatin-green finches
fidget in their huge cage.

Fritz flits with them.

4. Special Effects

Mud season: road melt: mastodons
lie down and blend with water.

Academy Awards:
Who will clench the statuette?

Look, the sickroom
is the school for cinema-horror.

Our hero is a pterosaur spent
from the hunt.

We kiss, glove up,
pump sleep in the shunt.

5. Sharp Reports

Listen to the ice *go out*.
Slab-continents explode
below the window.

Our Buddhists say his soul
is in the air.

On the bridge
between two states
I toss to ice floes

three dozen orchids
from G-d knows where:

six lovely testicles
per stem,.and trail

magenta down toward
the nuclear power plant.

OUR FALL

1.

September. The ferry from Weehawken
skirted Manhattan. Bathed in the light
of recent events, I saw the breach,
the wide berth, un-scraped sky,
smoke televised on the jittery Hudson.
Beauty shamed and stunned.

I joined a swarm around Zero's
powder-blue barricades.
Scanned photographs,
antiqued by longing, tore:

my brother commuted by water,
had inched *that close*…and…

Blocks away, a lacy structure
thundered down. Cranes bent
to the mound again. Soot underscored
the etiquette of guard to throngs—

Ladies and Gentlemen, please
shoot once and move on.

2.

Vermont. We caught our breath
in the forest clambered over
ruins, old logging traces, silted wells,

untimbered hearths
and pocketed souvenirs:

aqua jar glass stretched by fire,
iron hooks and eyes
unlatched from luck.

And fungus— after a single deluge,
deluxe gold lobes studded the deadfall:
Chicken of the Woods.

Dirty, dotty marshmallows
of *aborted entoloma*,
plump under leaf litter.

I pulled them loose, filled two shirts,
and crowed all the way to the car.

3.

The frigid orchard, a stone's throw
from Eden, Northern Spies shake down

for my final pie. In the glass house
of our safety, I pare this precious fruit.

Stove waves to radio,
shoe bomb, friendly fire,
softened strongholds.

I cut rot, core, and sample
noon's lethal truth.

Time takes no prisoners or blame.

Inches from the storm,
pegged to the cactus shelf,

our dormant garden gloves
touch palms—

divers, lovers
delve or pray.

AS TOPAZ BLAZES THROUGH BAGHDAD

We march and gnash our tears.

Old friends slog through Sunday mud
to the Franklin sugar house.
Late cold, tepid nights,
unstable season.

His red shirt blurred in a sweet cloud,
Dave calls *Hi.* Feeds slabs into fire,
and draws off viscous gold.

To peace! We pass
a tiny Dixie cup.

This week at the rifle range,
machine-gunners
new to the nuclear power plant
train again.

All day their "blam-blam"
drowns out trills and pings,

those drops in the bucket
we call Spring.

LUCK TREK

Christian says—
For luck all year, catch
twelve leaves before they land.

In her old country they believed
in leaves, chased Providence
through fall's funnel, spiral, whorl.

We climb past retentive trees—
no hand-out—to the local shrine
where tinted flags, Tibetan send-ups,
un-weft their scripture.

Wind tosses off our lips
aromatic synonyms
for gold and brown.
Look down now:
a lap robe, an afghan.

Afghanistan. War grinds stone.
Jets spit yellow rations
of grain and sorrow.

O, may she shuck the burqa
with its woven script,
and slip into the century
she's chosen?

I have nothing to offer
but luck:
a dozen leaves
before dark.

FALL BACKWARD

> on my birthday,
> election '04

Ohio spoke.
Worlds of wanwood leafmeal lie
neglected in my yard.

Ankle-deep, with odd,
undaunted joy, I rake
democracy:

Wind treats the trees:
maple, apple, willow, sumac.
Rain turns a trick.

Blood and gold
change hands.

Patriarch and sapling drop
their values; strip
to bathe without shame
or umbrage.

I'm raking in

the rain, wealth from any
cloud or branch.
Each bamboo sweep is
a swing-state avalanche.

Spread hope, the blue tarp,
under my poem.

THANKSGIVING: FOUR TO SIX A.M.

Double-take in the dark.
Sleet needles me
un-knits my sleep: it's that *tick*
below think itch within speech
the *tsk* of task.

Ice seeps back to rain—
Won't coat a stick
slur a wheel.
Two fluorescent hunters
cruise toward dawn
in a bronze Dart.
A hip flask loosens their intent.

The cats yowl for tinned meat
while rodents drunk on compost
snicker by the chimney.
In this sumac-red farmhouse
my young sack out
and I'm easy: *la-de-dah*
no axe to grind.

Day takes shape:
boughs bear globes
of pop-it beads
pretty and cheap.

Swank heat blows up
the grates: propane
Yahweh made
invisible and full of himself
comes clear from elsewhere
pricey as love or war.

BETHEL BREAKDOWN

Snow squall. Sickle moon.
Our first coat of winter is fun-
fur, cruelty-free, says the radio
embedded in my dash.

White thickens the road
I trace as tank and mortar soften-
up a city (one that rhymes
with *hallelujah*;) stone
vulnerable as snow.

Poof! My auto blows a gasket.
Smoke steams. I pull into
the white weeds. Flag down
a stranger. Surrender.

Radiator full: the water of
human kindness, I coast into a Shell:
no service, just convenience.
Punch the cell.
--Honey I am stranded.

Wrecker kid drives a resplendent rig;
lifts my strapped wheels to his iron bed.
Life heaves. My broad-leaf sage,
a garden gift, tilts into the backseat
heap of unrecycled ambushes.

Sage lends a dry serenity
to awe and woe. Page one:
Aurora borealis bruise blue and plum.
Fallujah: jittery specialists
hang rosaries on guns.

SONG OF THE UNINSURED

Uninsured though able for the moment
my body and I roll into "golden age."

It's passing strange: the vehicle and home
I shuttle from have coverage—

Whack a fender, trip and fracture
on my premises: adjusters gauge the damage

you endure and dole out a sum.
Rest assured, I pay. I pay the premium.

Listen, my body's coverage is skin.
Thick or thin, my only coverage is skin.

Calculate the odds I gamble on: my heart,
a slot machine, my dice, the density of bone;

the fear: a rhyme for "answer,"
the care I may postpone.

Risk is the lien on all I own or owe.
Luck is my doctor: touch and go.

FAREWELL

Separation is our state:
no country for the faint of heart.

Chart the miles a pencil travels.
Vowel and phrase acquaint the heart.

Mouth of ocean, vein of river,
ribs of cloud restrain the heart.

Wind and ice unite the dark.
If stars ignite the pane, take heart.

Ink tattoos the skin of paper.
Roll up a sleeve and paint your heart.

Distance is a dance, Verandah.
Earth is our remaindered heart.

EARLY PRAISE FOR *SUDDEN EDEN*

Neither the beauty nor the brokenness of the world escapes Verandah Porche's grasp in her newest collection, *Sudden Eden*. The orchard and the neighbor's homely sayings share equally with time and eternity. She is a wise poet who knows her land and its neighbors and the deeper truths of living a rural life in which "Late fruit/keeps its edge as frost/fleeces the pasture." These poems are about the investments one makes in life, in its loves and causes, its earth and trees, its human community. – **Maxine Chernoff,** *The Turning, Among the Names, World: Poems 1991-2001; Japan; Evolution of the Bridge: Selected Prose Poems,* and others.

Sudden Eden is a splendid collection of poems. Porche's tone is ingenuous yet sophisticated at once. The sections develop their own themes with style and forms to match; and grow to a wonderful climax. Formal trials are made with brisk clarity. But quiet melodies of inspired thought throughout make a more memorable achievement. Darts of lyric employing various devices hit bulls-eye after bulls-eye without apparent labor. Here's no chipping and chattering from classes; poems sail, unchided by the workshop. It's all Porche: perky, insouciant, blushing. Her wit shows us "the five o'clock shadow / of July and August" or "Baby weighs me down like a gallon of milk." There's more: reliable knowledge of country matters: "some legal country crop with a joke name / like shiitake mushrooms" or the colorful anecdotes in "100 Years of Squares and Reels." Space lacks to note all the accomplishments of this book. Many strong poems, for example "Thanksgiving, Four to Six A.M.," "Blue Seal," "First Cutting," "Nocturne," or "To Hell in a Handbasket" deserve to be read, reread and cherished. Images such as "Varicose skies" or keen similes ("late clouds / drift apart like marriages") abound. This collection deserves a prize. The wonders of her voice, her strong knowing and tender feelings, are just my cup of mead. – **Stephen Sandy**, *Circular Drives; Survivor, Walking; Huang's Tao Te Ching; The Inn at the Beginning Bar and Grill,* and others.

Out of her densely packed words and striking images – "two dotted U's" are breasts, a "Chanterelle: a trill of thrush made edible," "Ten below/the trees play air/guitar " – comes the story of her life, past generations back to Russia, her mother, father, the seasons, homesteading, children, the life of a working poet, other people's stories, lives, politics, joy and sorrow. It's all here. These are poems – both tough and tender and in many forms – of family, reminiscence: in sum an autobiography of a life well lived, and all of it totally engaging, important and well worth anyone's time. – **David Budbill**, *Happy Life, While We've Still Got Feet, Moment to Moment: Poems of a Mountain Recluse; Judevine; From Down to the Village*, and others.

This book, among other things, is a fitting testimony to Verandah Porche's longtime service as what I will call a poetry missionary, teaching the value – nay the centrality – of the poetic experience to people young and old, both in her home state of Vermont and elsewhere. Her collection, *Sudden Eden,* is cause for celebration. – **Syd Lea**, Vermont Poet Laureate, *Six Sundays; Toward a Seventh: Selected Spiritual Poems, Young of the Year; A Hundred Himalayas; To the Bone,* and others.

Further praise for *Sudden Eden*:

Like many kids who grew up in the Northeast, I first met Verandah Porche as a grade schooler – she came to our school to show us how words can paint pictures, how they can make you laugh or ache, remember or imagine. Language as song, as prayer, even as math. How language can stimulate the senses – even touch, as certain words can feel physically pleasurable as they roll of your tongue. – **Dave Mance III**, Editor, *Northern Woodland*.

About the author:

Verandah Porche works as a poet-in-residence, performer and writing partner. Based in rural Vermont since 1968, she has published *The Body's Symmetry* (Harper and Row) and *Glancing Off* (See Through Books), and has pursued an alternative literary career, creating collaborative writing projects in nontraditional settings: literacy and crisis centers, hospitals, factories, nursing homes, senior centers, a 200-year-old Vermont tavern and an urban working class neighborhood. *Broad Brook Anthology*, a play for voices, honors the lives of elders in Guilford, Vermont. *Listening Out Loud* documents her residency with Real Art Ways in Hartford, CT.

As Muse for Hire. she writes poems for moments or milestones in the lives of friends and strangers. "Come Over" is a cd of songs written with Patty Carpenter, performed by the Dysfunctional Family Jazz band. She has read her work on NPR stations, at the Palace of Friendship in the former Leningrad and at the John Simon Guggenheim Museum. The Vermont Arts Council presented her with its Award of Merit in 1998 and Marlboro College awarded Ms. Porche an honorary Doctor of Humane Letters in 2012.

Thanks to the Vermont Arts Council and the National Endowment for the Arts for generous support.

National Endowment for the Arts